MAKING
BREAD

~ M A K I N G ~
BREAD
the taste of traditional home-baking

LORENZ BOOKS

This edition published by Lorenz Books
an imprint of
Anness Publishing Limited
Hermes House
88-89 Blackfriars Road
London SE1 8HA

This edition distributed in Canada by Raincoast Books,
8680 Cambie Street, Vancouver, British Columbia V6P 6M9

A CIP catalogue record for this book is available from the
British Library

Publisher: Joanna Lorenz
Senior Cookery Editor: Linda Fraser
Series Editor: Sarah Ainley
Copy Editor: Jenni Fleetwood
Designers: Patrick McLeavey & Partners
Illustrator: Anna Koska
Photographers: Karl Adamson, Edward Allright, Steve Baxter, James Duncan,
Michelle Garrett, Amanda Heywood, Michael Michaels & Don Last
Recipes: Alex Baxter, Jacqueline Clark, Carole Clements, Joanna Farrow,
Rafi Fernandez, Shirley Gill, Christine France & Elizabeth Wolf-Cohen

© Anness Publishing Limited 1998
Updated © 2000
1 3 5 7 9 10 8 6 4 2

For all recipes, quantities are given in both metric and imperial measures,
and, where appropriate, measures are also given in standard
cups and spoons. Follow one set, but not a mixture, because
they are not interchangeable.

Contents

Introduction

There can be few aromas as tantalizing as that of baking bread. Bottle it and you would make a fortune, but buyers would miss out on so much: the pleasure of 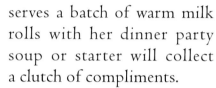 pummelling the dough, the satisfaction of seeing it rise and the feeling of triumph when golden loaves emerge fresh from the oven. And then there's the ultimate enjoyment: the moment when you take your first delicious bite of bread you've baked yourself.

But is it worth it — when you can so easily pop down to the supermarket or bakery and bring back a bloomer or a cottage loaf? Yes, it is. Not for every day, perhaps, but for special occasions there's nothing like home baking. House guests will rise early if home-made croissants are on the breakfast menu, and the cook who serves a batch of warm milk rolls with her dinner party soup or starter will collect a clutch of compliments.

The French have always given bread the status it deserves, appreciating it not merely for its food value, but as the best way to mop up every last trace of gravy or sauce on the plate. How sensible, how satisfying! And, from the cook's point of view, how simple. Serve a fine beef stew, packed with vegetables in a rich wine or brandy-flavoured stock, and all you need is a fresh crusty loaf and the company of friends for a perfect meal.

If you've never baked your own bread, perhaps under the mistaken impression that it is difficult, or troublesome, or best left to the experts, you will find this book invaluable. Every recipe uses easy-blend dried yeast, which instantly takes the mystique out of mastering this ancient art. Easy-blend yeast comes in sealed foil sachets, so it stays fresh until it is needed. It is added directly to the flour mixture, so there's no need to mix with milk and sugar and wait for the froth, fearful that you've overheated the liquid and killed off the yeast. Baking bread used to be a bit like bathing a baby — much anxious testing was required to make sure the water was neither too hot nor too cold. With easy-blend yeast hand-hot liquid is advised, but the temperature is not as crucial a factor as it once was.

The most important part of baking bread is the kneading of the dough. The dough has to be well kneaded to allow the gluten to fully develop. Give it ten minutes of strenuous action and the results will be impressive.

Dough made with easy-blend yeast only needs a single rising, which saves time and effort. Allow longer for rich doughs, as the addition of sugar, butter and eggs slows down the action of the yeast. Corn Bread is leavened with baking powder, while Sage Soda Bread makes use of the special properties of its ingredients, buttermilk and baking soda.

On the sweeter side, there are plenty of tasty treats in store in this collection to tempt you into the kitchen. From Plaited Prune Bread to Date & Pecan Loaf, teabreads, breadsticks, brioches and rolls — they are rising stars, every one!

Breadmaking Ingredients

FLOUR

For yeast breads, use white flour. Whether you use self-raising or plain flour depends on the recipe. White flour has a high gluten content, absorbs water readily and produces an elastic dough when kneaded. Wholemeal flour needs to be kneaded well, while loaves made with rye flour are denser. Cornmeal makes a very good quick bread.

8

YEAST

All recipes in this book use easy-blend dried yeast, which is added directly to the dry ingredients. The dough generally needs a single rising. If you use fresh yeast, blend it with warm liquid in a jug, leave until frothy, then add to the dry ingredients in a bowl. Prove the dough twice, first in the bowl, then again after shaping.

OTHER LEAVENERS

Baking powder is an effective raising agent when added to plain flour. Bicarbonate of soda needs an acid such as buttermilk to activate it. Both start to work as soon as they are combined with the liquid, so cook the mixture immediately after mixing.

SALT

An essential ingredient in yeast breads, salt stops the yeast from working too quickly.

SUGAR

A little sugar added to fresh yeast gives it a good start, but it is not necessary to add it to easy-blend dried yeast, since yeast converts starch in the flour to sugar. Too much sugar slows down the action of the yeast, so rich sweet doughs may need more yeast and a longer rising time.

FAT

Adding oil, butter or margarine to a dough improves the softness of the crumb and delays staleness. Don't add too much, or the action of the yeast will be impaired.

LIQUID

Water is the liquid most often used in breadmaking. Amounts stated in recipes are approximate as flours vary in how much liquid they absorb. Always use hand-hot water with easy-blend dried yeast.

EGGS

Eggs add flavour and colour to the dough. They also boost the nutritional value and improve the keeping quality of rich breads.

DRIED FRUIT

Sweet yeast doughs and teabreads often contain raisins, sultanas, peel or currants. Snipped ready-to-eat dried apricots, peaches and apples are also excellent. Knead them thoroughly into the dough.

NUTS

Almonds, hazelnuts, walnuts and pecan nuts add wonderful texture and flavour. Swirl finely chopped nuts through dough twists, or use them for a topping.

VEGETABLES

Lightly fried onions or celery are delicious in savoury breads, as are spinach, courgettes and sun-dried tomatoes.

SEEDS

Sesame, poppy and caraway seeds make marvellous toppings. Cardamom seeds are sometimes added to savoury doughs.

HERBS AND SPICES

Savoury doughs often include fresh or dried herbs, while spices like cinnamon and nutmeg give a warm taste to sweet doughs.

CHEESE

A small amount of mature Cheddar or Parmesan adds flavour without increasing the fat content of dough too much. Grated cheese can also be used as a topping.

9

Techniques

USING EASY-BLEND DRIED YEAST

Do not mix the yeast with liquid but add straight from the sachet to dry ingredients. Use hand-hot liquid for mixing the dough. Knead well. The dough will only need a single rising.

USING DRIED YEAST

Sprinkle the yeast on to lukewarm liquid. Add a pinch of sugar. Stir, then set aside until frothy. Add to the dry ingredients and knead well. Prove in the bowl and again after shaping.

USING FRESH YEAST

Crumble fresh yeast into a small bowl and add a pinch of sugar. Cream the mixture with a little lukewarm water, then set aside in a warm place until frothy. Prove the dough once in the bowl, then once again after shaping.

ADDING FATS

Diced butter or margarine may be added to the dry ingredients. Rub the fat between your fingertips until the mixture resembles breadcrumbs. If oil is used, add it with the liquid.

KNEADING THE DOUGH

To develop the gluten and ensure a good rise, knead the dough thoroughly for 10 minutes on a lightly floured surface. Fold the dough towards you, then push it down firmly and away with the heel of your hand. Turn the dough. Repeat the action until the dough feels smooth, elastic and no longer sticky.

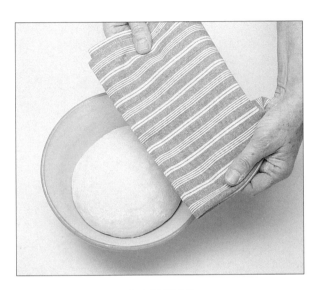

SHAPING ROLLS

Cottage Rolls: Shape two-thirds of the dough into rounds, about the size of golf balls. Shape the rest of the dough into smaller rounds. Make a dent in each large ball and centre a small ball on top. Push a lightly floured index finger through the middle of both dough balls to join them.

Knots: Roll each dough portion to a fairly thin sausage shape. Carefully knot the dough, as you would a piece of string.

Twists: Twist two strands of dough together, dampen the ends and press them together firmly to hold the shape.

Cloverleaf Rolls: Divide each portion of dough into three equal pieces. Dampen them lightly and fit the pieces together in a bun tin. Press together lightly to hold.

PROVING

This term describes setting the dough aside to rise. Doughs made with easy-blend yeast only need to be proved once, whereas doughs made with other forms of yeast are proved in the bowl and once again after the dough has been shaped. Proving times will vary according to the amount of dough and the ambient temperature. Keep the dough moist by covering it with a clean tea towel or lightly oiled plastic wrap (or slip the tin into a plastic bag, ballooning it to trap the air). Leave in a warm place for an hour or until doubled in bulk. Dough will rise in a fridge but will take much longer.

Classic Breads

White Bread

INGREDIENTS

25g / 1oz / 2 tbsp butter
475ml / 16fl oz / 2 cups milk
800g / 1¾lb / 7 cups strong white flour
10ml / 2 tsp salt
5ml / 1 tsp caster sugar
15ml / 1 tbsp easy-blend dried yeast
beaten egg, for glazing

MAKES 2 LOAVES

1 Melt the butter in the milk in a saucepan. Pour into a jug and cool to hand-hot. Sift the flour into a large mixing bowl and stir in the salt, caster sugar and yeast. Make a well in the centre and add the milk mixture. Mix to a soft dough.

2 Lightly grease two 450g/1lb loaf tins. Knead the dough on a lightly floured surface for about 10 minutes or until it is smooth and elastic. Divide the dough  in half, shape each half into a loaf shape and place in the prepared loaf tins.

3 Slip the tins into a large, lightly oiled plastic bag and leave them to rise in a warm place for about 1 hour or until the loaves have doubled in bulk.

4 Preheat the oven to 200°C/400°F/Gas 6. Glaze the loaves with beaten egg and bake for 40–45 minutes or until well risen and golden brown. Turn out and cool on a wire rack.

13

Plaited Loaf

INGREDIENTS

50g / 2oz / ¼ cup butter
250ml / 8fl oz / 1 cup milk
5ml / 1 tsp clear honey
450g / 1lb / 4 cups strong white flour
5ml / 1 tsp salt
15ml / 1 tbsp easy-blend dried yeast
1 egg, lightly beaten
1 egg yolk beaten with 5ml / 1 tsp milk,
for glazing

MAKES 1 LOAF

1 Melt the butter in the milk in a saucepan. Stir in the honey until dissolved. Pour into a jug and set aside to cool to hand-hot.

2 Sift the flour into a large mixing bowl and stir in the salt and yeast. Make a well in the centre. Add the hand-hot milk mixture and the egg. Mix to a rough dough.

3 Transfer the dough to a lightly floured surface and knead until smooth and elastic. Divide the dough into three equal pieces. Roll each piece into a long, thin strip.

4 Grease a baking sheet. Plait the three strips of dough loosely on the baking sheet. Tuck the ends of the strips under the plait to make a neat finish.

5 Cover the plait loosely and leave to rise in a warm place for about 1 hour, until doubled in bulk. Preheat the oven to 190°C/375°F/Gas 5.

6 Brush the loaf with the glaze and bake for 40–45 minutes until golden. The loaf should sound hollow when rapped underneath. Remove from the baking sheet with a fish slice and allow to cool on a wire rack.

COOK'S TIP

An easy way to make the plait is to begin by placing two dough strips together in the shape of a cone or tent. At the point where they meet, add the third strip so that the shape now looks like a tripod. Starting with the left strip, plait the dough loosely.

French Bread

INGREDIENTS

800g–1.2kg/1¾–2½lb/7–10 cups strong
white flour
15ml/1 tbsp salt
15ml/1 tbsp easy-blend dried yeast
475ml/16fl oz/2 cups hand-hot water
semolina or plain flour, for dusting baking sheet

MAKES 2 LOAVES

1 Mix 800g/1¾lb/7 cups of the flour with the salt and yeast in a bowl. Pour the hand-hot water into a mixing bowl. Beat in the flour mixture, about 115g/4oz/1 cup at a time, to make a smooth dough. If necessary, add the rest of the flour.

2 Transfer the dough to a lightly floured surface and knead until smooth and elastic. Divide in half and shape into two long loaves. Dust a baking  sheet with semolina or flour, place the loaves on top and cover loosely. Leave in a warm place to rise for about 1 hour or until doubled in bulk.

3 Score the tops of the sticks with a sharp knife. Brush with water and place in a cold oven. Place a roasting tin half-filled with boiling water on the bottom of the oven.

4 Set the oven to 200°C/400°F/Gas 6. Bake the loaves for about 40 minutes. Cool on a wire rack.

Sesame Seed Bread

INGREDIENTS

175g/6oz/1½ cups plain white flour
175g/6oz/1½ cups wholemeal flour
5ml/1 tsp salt
10ml/2 tsp easy-blend dried yeast
300ml/½ pint/1¼ cups hand-hot water
25g/1oz/½ cup toasted sesame seeds
milk, for glazing
30ml/2 tbsp sesame seeds, for sprinkling

MAKES 1 LOAF

4 Glaze the loaf with the milk. Sprinkle with the sesame seeds. Bake for 15 minutes, then lower the oven temperature to 190°C/375°F/Gas 5 and bake for

about 30 minutes more, until the loaf is golden and sounds hollow when rapped underneath. Cool on a wire rack.

1 Sift the flours into a large mixing bowl, then stir in the salt and yeast. Make a well in the centre and stir in enough of the hand-hot water to make a rough dough.

2 Knead the dough on a lightly floured surface for 10 minutes, or until smooth and elastic. Knead in the sesame seeds until evenly distributed.

3 Grease a 23cm/9in cake tin. Divide the dough into 16 balls and fit them side by side in the tin. Cover with a lightly oiled plastic bag and leave in a warm place for about 1 hour, or until the loaf has risen to above the rim of the tin. Preheat the oven to 220°C/425°F/Gas 7.

Corn Bread

INGREDIENTS

115g/4oz/1 cup plain flour
75g/3oz/6 tbsp caster sugar
5ml/1 tsp salt
15ml/1 tbsp baking powder
175g/6oz/1½ cups cornmeal (polenta)
350ml/12fl oz/1½ cups milk
2 eggs
75g/3oz/6 tbsp butter, melted
115g/4oz/½ cup solid margarine, melted

MAKES 1 LOAF

1 Preheat the oven to 200°C/400°F/Gas 6. Grease a 450g/1lb loaf tin. Line the base with non-stick baking paper.

2 Sift the flour, sugar, salt and baking powder into a large mixing bowl. Stir in the cornmeal. Make a well in the centre of the flour with a wooden spoon.

3 Whisk the milk and eggs with the melted butter and margarine until well combined. Pour the mixture into the well in the flour mixture. Stir until just blended; do not overmix or the cooked bread will not be light.

4 Pour into the prepared tin and bake for about 45 minutes, or until a skewer inserted in the centre of the loaf comes out clean. Turn on to a wire rack. Serve hot or at room temperature. The bread makes an excellent accompaniment to a Mexican meal.

Wholemeal Bread

INGREDIENTS

450ml / ¾ pint / 1¾ cups water
30ml / 2 tbsp clear honey
550g / 1lb 5oz / 5¼ cups wholemeal flour
10ml / 2 tsp salt
20ml / 4 tsp easy-blend dried yeast
40g / 1½oz / ¾ cup wheatgerm
45ml / 3 tbsp corn oil
milk, for glazing

MAKES 1 LOAF

1 Heat the water in a small pan to simmering point. Stir in the honey until dissolved. Pour into a jug and cool to hand-hot.

2 Combine the flour, salt, yeast and wheatgerm in a mixing bowl. Make a well in the centre and pour in the oil, with enough liquid to make a soft dough.

3 Lightly grease a 450g/1lb loaf tin. Knead the dough on a lightly floured surface for 10 minutes. Shape into a loaf and place in the prepared tin. Slip the tin into a lightly oiled plastic bag and leave the loaf to rise in a warm place for about 1 hour or until doubled in bulk. Preheat the oven to 200°C/400°F/Gas 6.

4 Glaze the loaf with the milk. Bake for 35–40 minutes until the crust is golden brown. The loaf should sound hollow when rapped underneath. Allow to cool on a wire rack.

19

Rye Bread

INGREDIENTS

475ml/16fl oz/2 cups water
30ml/2 tbsp molasses
350g/12oz/3 cups wholemeal flour
225g/8oz/2 cups rye flour
115g/4oz/1 cup strong white flour
7.5ml/1½ tsp salt
10g/¼oz sachet easy-blend dried yeast
30ml/2 tbsp caraway seeds
30ml/2 tbsp sunflower oil

MAKES 2 LOAVES

1 Heat the water in a small pan to simmering point. Stir in the molasses until dissolved. Pour into a jug and cool to hand-hot.

2 Sift the three types of flour into a large mixing bowl. Stir in the salt and yeast. Set 5ml/1 tsp of the caraway seeds aside and add the rest to the bowl.

3 Make a well in the centre. Then add the oil, with enough of the hand-hot liquid to make a soft dough. Add a little more of the liquid if necessary.

4 Knead the dough on a lightly floured surface for 10 minutes, until smooth and elastic. Divide in half and shape each piece to a 23cm/9in long oval loaf.

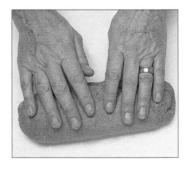

5 Grease a large baking sheet. Put the loaves on the sheet, leaving room for rising. Flatten them slightly. Slide the baking sheet into a lightly oiled large plastic bag and leave in a warm place for up to 2 hours, until the dough has doubled in bulk. Preheat the oven to 200°C/400°F/Gas 6.

6 Brush the loaves with water and sprinkle with the reserved caraway seeds. Bake for 30 minutes or until well risen. The loaves should sound hollow when rapped underneath. Cool on a wire rack.

20

Three-grain Bread

INGREDIENTS

475ml/16fl oz/2 cups water
30ml/2 tbsp malt extract
225g/8oz/2 cups strong white flour
225g/8oz/2 cups malted brown flour
225g/8oz/2 cups rye flour
7.5ml/1½ tsp salt
15ml/1 tbsp easy-blend dried yeast
30ml/2 tbsp linseed
75g/3oz/¾ cup medium oatmeal
45ml/3 tbsp sunflower seeds

MAKES 1 LOAF

22

1 Heat the water in a small pan to simmering point. Stir in the malt extract until dissolved. Pour into a jug and cool to hand-hot.

2 Sift the three types of flour into a large mixing bowl. Stir in the salt and yeast. Set aside 5ml/1 tsp of the linseed and add the rest to the flour mixture with  the oatmeal and sunflower seeds. Using a wooden spoon, mix together well.

3 Make a well in the centre of the flour mixture. Add the hand-hot liquid and mix to a soft dough, adding more white flour if needed. Knead on a lightly 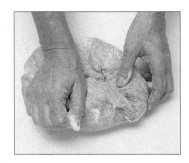 floured surface for 10 minutes, or until smooth and elastic.

4 Lightly grease a large baking sheet. Divide the dough in half. Roll each half to a 30cm/12in sausage. Twist the sausages together, dampen the ends and press to seal.

5 Place the twist on the prepared baking sheet, sprinkle with the remaining linseed and cover loosely. Leave in a warm place for 2 hours, or until the dough has doubled in bulk. Preheat the oven to 220°C/425°F/Gas 7.

6 Bake the loaf for 10 minutes, then lower the oven temperature to 200°C/400°F/Gas 6 and cook for 20 minutes more. Allow to cool on a wire rack.

Herb &
Savoury Breads

Spiral Herb Bread

INGREDIENTS

350g/12oz/3 cups strong white flour
350g/12oz/3 cups wholemeal flour
15ml/1 tbsp salt
2 x 10g/¼oz sachets easy-blend dried yeast
600ml/1 pint/2½ cups hand-hot water
25g/1oz/2 tbsp butter
1 bunch spring onions, finely chopped
1 garlic clove, crushed
1 large bunch fresh parsley, finely chopped
salt and ground black pepper
milk, for glazing

MAKES 2 LOAVES

1 Sift the flours into a large mixing bowl, then stir in the salt and yeast. Make a well in the centre and add enough of the hand-hot water to make a rough dough. Knead on a lightly floured surface for 10 minutes, or until smooth and elastic.

2 Melt the butter in a small frying pan and fry the spring onions and garlic until soft. Stir in the chopped fresh parsley, with salt and pepper to taste.

3 Lightly grease two 450g/1lb loaf tins. Divide the dough in half. Roll out each piece in turn to a 35 x 23cm/14 x 9in rectangle. Spread each rectangle with half the herb mixture, taking it just to the edges of the dough.

4 Roll up each rectangle loosely from a short side. Pinch the ends to seal. Place each roll in a loaf tin, cover loosely and leave to rise in a warm place for about 1 hour, until the loaves have doubled in bulk. Preheat the oven to 190°C/375°F/Gas 5.

5 Glaze the loaves with milk. Bake for about 50 minutes or until they sound hollow when rapped underneath. Cool on a wire rack.

25

Rosemary Bread

INGREDIENTS

25g/1oz/2 tbsp butter
300ml/½ pint/1¼ cups milk
175g/6oz/1½ cups white self-raising flour
175g/6oz/1½ cups wholemeal flour
15ml/1 tbsp caster sugar
5ml/1 tsp salt
10g/¼oz sachet easy-blend dried yeast
15ml/1 tbsp sesame seeds
15ml/1 tbsp dried chopped onion
15ml/1 tbsp chopped fresh rosemary leaves
115g/4oz/1 cup mature Cheddar cheese, cubed
coarse sea salt and rosemary sprigs, to garnish

MAKES 1 LOAF

1 Melt the butter in the milk in a small saucepan. Cool the mixture to hand-hot. Combine both types of flour with the sugar, salt and yeast in a large mixing bowl. Make a well in the centre.

2 Add the milk mixture, with the sesame seeds, dried chopped onion and rosemary leaves. Mix to a dough, then knead on a lightly floured surface until smooth.

3 Flatten the dough, then add the cheese cubes. Knead in until well distributed. Lightly grease a 450g/1lb loaf tin. Shape the dough into a loaf, place it in the tin and cover loosely. Leave to rise in a warm place for about 1 hour, until doubled in bulk. Preheat the oven to 190°C/375°F/Gas 5.

4 Bake the loaf for 30 minutes, covering it with foil towards the end of cooking if it starts to become too brown. Cool on a wire rack. Scatter coarse sea salt and a few rosemary sprigs on top to serve.

Sage Soda Bread

INGREDIENTS

225g / 8oz / 2 cups wholemeal flour
115g / 4oz / 1 cup strong white flour
2.5ml / ½ tsp salt
5ml / 1 tsp bicarbonate of soda
30ml / 2 tbsp shredded fresh sage leaves
300–450ml / ½–¾ pint / 1¼–1¾
cups buttermilk

MAKES 1 LOAF

1 Preheat the oven to 220°C/425°F/ Gas 7. Lightly oil a baking sheet. Sift both types of flour into a bowl, then tip in any bran remaining in the sieve. Stir in the salt, bicarbonate of soda and sage.

2 Add enough of the buttermilk to make a soft dough, mixing just enough to combine the ingredients. Shape the dough into a round and place on the baking sheet.

3 Cut a deep cross in the top of the loaf. Bake for 40 minutes or until the loaf is well risen and sounds hollow when rapped underneath. Cool on a wire rack. Serve warm, with butter.

27

Olive & Oregano Bread

INGREDIENTS

15ml / 1 tbsp olive oil
1 onion, finely chopped
*450g / 1lb / 4 cups strong white flour, plus
extra for dusting*
5ml / 1 tsp salt
1.5ml / 1/4 tsp ground black pepper
5ml / 1 tsp easy-blend dried yeast
*50g / 2oz / 1/3 cup stoned black olives,
roughly chopped*
15ml / 1 tbsp black olive paste
15ml / 1 tbsp chopped fresh oregano
15ml / 1 tbsp chopped fresh parsley
300ml / 1/2 pint / 1 1/4 cups hand-hot water

MAKES 1 LOAF

28

1 Heat the olive oil in a frying pan. Add the onion and fry over a medium heat for 4–5 minutes, until golden. Grease a large baking sheet.

2 Sift the flour and salt into a large mixing bowl. Stir in the pepper and yeast. Make a well in the centre and add the fried onion (with the cooking oil), olives, olive paste and herbs. Stir in enough of the hand-hot water to make a soft dough, adding a little more water if necessary.

3 Transfer the dough to a lightly floured surface and knead for 10 minutes, until smooth and elastic. Shape to a 20cm/8in round and place on the prepared baking sheet.

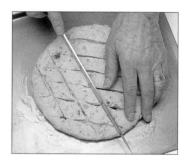

4 Using a sharp knife, make criss-cross cuts over the top of the dough. Slip the baking sheet into a lightly oiled plastic bag and leave the loaf to rise in a warm place for about 1 hour, until doubled in bulk. Preheat the oven to 220°C/425°F/Gas 7.

5 Dust the loaf with a little flour. Bake for 10 minutes, then lower the oven temperature to 200°C/400°F/Gas 6 and bake for 20 minutes more. The loaf is ready when it sounds hollow when rapped underneath. Cool the loaf slightly on a wire rack. Serve warm.

COOK'S TIP

This bread is delicious served with minestrone or a simple tomato and mozzarella salad.

Dill Bread

INGREDIENTS

60ml/4 tbsp olive oil
½ onion, chopped
800–900g/1¾–2lb/7–8 cups strong white flour
10ml/2 tsp salt
15ml/1 tbsp caster sugar
2 x 10g/¼oz sachets easy-blend dried yeast
1 large bunch dill, finely chopped
2 eggs, lightly beaten
115g/4oz/½ cup cottage cheese
475ml/16fl oz/2 cups hand-hot water
milk, for glazing

MAKES 2 LOAVES

1 Heat 15ml/1 tbsp of the olive oil in a small frying pan and fry the onion until soft. Set aside to cool. Lightly grease a large baking sheet.

2 Combine the flour, salt, sugar and yeast in a large mixing bowl. Make a well in the centre and add the onion (with the cooking oil), dill, eggs, cottage cheese and remaining oil. Stir in enough of the hand-hot water to make a soft dough.

3 Knead the dough on a lightly floured surface until smooth and elastic. Divide in half and shape each piece into a round.

4 Place the rounds of dough on the baking sheet, cover loosely and leave to rise in a warm place for about 1 hour or until doubled in bulk. Preheat the oven to 190°C/ 375°F/Gas 5.

5 Score the tops of the loaves, glaze with milk and bake for about 45 minutes, until browned. Allow the loaves to cool slightly on a wire rack before serving.

Courgette Crown Bread

INGREDIENTS

450g / 1lb courgettes
salt
500g / 1¼lb / 5 cups strong white flour
2 x 10g / ¼oz sachets easy-blend dried yeast
50g / 2oz / ⅔ cup grated Parmesan cheese
ground black pepper
30ml / 2 tbsp olive oil
300ml / ½ pint / 1¼ cups hand-hot water
milk, for glazing
sesame seeds, for the topping

MAKES 1 LOAF

4 Shape the dough into eight rolls. Fit them into the cake tin, brush the tops with the milk and sprinkle with sesame seeds. Allow the dough rolls to rise again.

5 Preheat the oven to 200°C/400°F/Gas 6. Bake the bread for 25 minutes or until golden brown. Cool on a wire rack.

31

1 Top and tail the courgettes, then grate them into a colander. Sprinkle each layer lightly with salt. Leave to drain for 30 minutes, then rinse, drain and pat dry.

2 Grease and base line a 23cm/9in round sandwich cake tin. Mix the flour, yeast and Parmesan in a large mixing bowl. Season with black pepper.

3 Stir in the oil and courgettes and add enough of the hand-hot water to make a fairly firm dough. Knead on a lightly floured surface for 10 minutes. Return to the clean bowl, cover and leave in a warm place to rise for 1 hour or until doubled in bulk.

Cheese Bread

INGREDIENTS

25g/1oz/2 tbsp butter
250ml/8fl oz/1 cup milk
350g/12oz/3 cups strong white flour
10ml/2 tsp salt
10g/¼oz sachet easy-blend dried yeast
115g/4oz/1 cup grated mature
Cheddar cheese

MAKES 1 LOAF

1 Melt the butter in the milk in a saucepan. Pour into a jug and cool to hand-hot. Sift the flour into a large mixing bowl and stir in the salt and yeast. Make a well in the centre and add the milk mixture. Mix to a soft dough.

2 Knead the dough on a lightly floured surface for 10 minutes, then pat it flat and sprinkle with the grated Cheddar cheese. Gather up the dough and knead again to distribute the cheese evenly.

3 Lightly grease a loaf tin. Twist the dough, form into a loaf shape and place in the tin, tucking the ends under. Cover loosely and leave in a warm place for about 1 hour, until doubled in bulk.

4 Preheat the oven to 200°C/400°F/Gas 6. Bake the loaf for 15 minutes, then lower the heat to 190°C/375°F/Gas 5 and bake for 20–30 minutes more, or until the bottom sounds hollow when rapped. Cool on a wire rack.

VARIATION
Try this recipe with grated Red Leicester cheese, Gruyère or Jarlsberg for a delicious alternative.

32

Parma Ham & Parmesan Bread

INGREDIENTS

225g/8oz/2 cups self-raising
wholemeal flour
225g/8oz/2 cups self-raising white flour
5ml/1 tsp baking powder
5ml/1 tsp salt
5ml/1 tsp ground black pepper
75g/3oz Parma ham, chopped
25g/1oz/⅓ cup grated Parmesan cheese
30ml/2 tbsp chopped fresh parsley
45ml/3 tbsp Meaux mustard
350ml/12fl oz/1½ cups buttermilk, plus
extra for glazing

MAKES 1 LOAF

1 Preheat the oven to 200°C/400°F/Gas 6. Lightly flour a baking sheet. Place the wholemeal flour in a bowl and sift in the white flour, baking powder and salt. Stir in the pepper and the ham. Set aside about 15ml/1 tbsp of the grated Parmesan and stir the rest into the mixture, with the parsley. Make a well in the centre.

2 Mix the mustard and buttermilk in a jug, pour on to the flour mixture and quickly mix to a soft dough. Knead briefly on a lightly floured surface, then shape the dough into an oval loaf.

3 Brush the loaf with buttermilk, sprinkle with the reserved Parmesan and place on the baking sheet. Bake for 25–30 minutes, or until golden brown. Cool on a wire rack.

COOK'S TIP

If you can't locate buttermilk, use lightly soured milk instead. Stir 5ml/1 tsp lemon juice into 350ml/12fl oz/1½ cups milk. Set aside for 15 minutes before use.

Spinach & Bacon Bread

INGREDIENTS

15ml/1 tbsp olive oil
1 onion, chopped
115g/4oz rindless smoked lean back bacon
rashers, chopped
225g/8oz chopped spinach, thawed if frozen
675g/1½lb/6 cups strong white flour
7.5ml/1½ tsp salt
10ml/¼oz sachet easy-blend dried yeast
2.5ml/½ tsp grated nutmeg
450ml/¾ pint/1¾ cups hand-hot water
25g/1oz/¼ cup grated mature
Cheddar cheese

MAKES 2 LOAVES

1 Heat the oil in a frying pan and fry the onion and chopped bacon for 5–8 minutes until golden brown (the bacon should not be crisp). If you are using thawed

frozen spinach, make sure it is thoroughly drained.

2 Sift the flour and salt into a large bowl. Add the yeast and nutmeg. Tip in the fried onion and bacon (with the cooking oil), then add the chopped

spinach and enough of the hand-hot water to make a soft dough.

3 Transfer the dough to a lightly floured surface and knead for about 10 minutes, or until the dough is smooth and elastic. Divide the dough in half and shape each piece into a ball.

4 Lightly grease two 23cm/9in sandwich cake tins. Flatten each dough ball slightly and place each ball in a greased tin, using your fingertips to extend the dough to the edges.

5 Mark each loaf into eight wedges and sprinkle with the cheese. Cover loosely with a lightly oiled plastic bag and leave in a warm place to rise for about 1 hour, or until doubled in bulk. Preheat the oven to 200°C/400°F/Gas 6.

6 Bake the loaves for 25–30 minutes, or until they sound hollow when rapped underneath. Cool slightly on a wire rack before serving.

Sun-dried Tomato Plait

INGREDIENTS

225g/8oz/2 cups wholemeal flour
225g/8oz/2 cups strong white flour
5ml/1 tsp salt
1.5ml/¼ tsp ground black pepper
10ml/2 tsp easy-blend dried yeast
25g/1oz/⅓ cup grated Parmesan cheese
30ml/2 tbsp red pesto
115g/4oz/⅔ cup drained sun-dried tomatoes
in oil, chopped, plus 15ml/1 tbsp oil
from the jar
300ml/½ pint/1¼ cups hand-hot water
5ml/1 tsp coarse sea salt, for sprinkling

MAKES 1 LOAF

1 Sift both types of flour into a mixing bowl, then tip in any bran remaining in the sieve. Stir in the salt, pepper and yeast. Make a well in the centre.

2 Add the Parmesan, pesto and chopped sun-dried tomatoes (with the oil) to the well in the dry ingredients, then stir in enough of the hand-hot water to make a soft dough. Add more water if necessary.

3 Transfer the dough to a lightly floured surface and knead for 10 minutes, until smooth and elastic. Divide into three equal pieces and roll each to a 33cm/13in long sausage.

4 Lightly grease a large baking sheet. Dampen the ends of the three pieces of dough. Press them together at one end, plait them loosely, then press them together at the other end to give a neat finish.

5 Place the plaited loaf on the baking sheet, cover with a lightly oiled plastic bag and leave to rise in a warm place for 1 hour, or until doubled in bulk. Preheat the oven to 220°C/425°F/Gas 7.

6 Sprinkle the plait with the coarse sea salt. Bake for 10 minutes, then lower the oven temperature to 200°C/400°F/Gas 6. Bake for 15–20 minutes more, or until the loaf sounds hollow when rapped underneath. Cool on a wire rack.

COOK'S TIP
If you can't find any red pesto, use 30ml/
2 tbsp snipped fresh basil mixed with
15ml/1 tbsp sun-dried tomato paste.

36

Fruit Breads & Teabreads

Raisin Bread

INGREDIENTS

175g/6oz/1 cup seedless raisins
75g/3oz/1/2 cup currants
15ml/1 tbsp brandy
2.5ml/1/2 tsp grated nutmeg
grated rind of 1 large orange
115g/4oz/1/2 cup butter
475ml/16fl oz/2 cups milk
675g/1 1/2lb/6 cups plain flour
5ml/1 tsp salt
75g/3oz/6 tbsp caster sugar
15ml/1 tbsp easy-blend dried yeast
1 egg beaten with 15ml/1 tbsp single cream,
for glazing

MAKES 2 LOAVES

1 Mix the dried fruit, brandy, nutmeg and orange rind in a bowl. Melt 50g/2oz/1/4 cup of the butter in the milk in a saucepan. Cool to hand-hot.

2 Sift the flour into a large mixing bowl and stir in the salt, sugar and yeast. Add the milk mixture and mix to a dough, then knead on a lightly floured surface for 10 minutes until smooth and elastic.

3 Grease two 450g/1lb loaf tins. Melt the remaining butter. Divide the dough in half. Roll each half to a rectangle measuring 50 x 20cm/20 x 8in.

4 Brush with the melted butter and sprinkle evenly with the raisin mixture. Roll up from a short side, tucking in the ends slightly. Place in the tins, cover and leave in a warm place to rise for about 1 1/2 hours or until doubled in bulk. Preheat the oven to 200°C/400°F/Gas 6.

5 Glaze the loaves with the egg and cream mixture. Bake for 20 minutes, then lower the oven temperature to 180°C/350°F/Gas 4 and bake for 20–25 minutes more, or until golden. Cool on wire racks.

Plaited Prune Bread

INGREDIENTS

50g/2oz/¼ cup butter
60ml/4 tbsp milk
450g/1lb/4 cups plain flour
2.5ml/½ tsp salt
50g/2oz/¼ cup caster sugar
10g/¼oz sachet easy-blend dried yeast
1 egg, lightly beaten
60ml/4 tbsp hand-hot water
1 egg, beaten with 10ml/2 tsp
water, for glazing
FILLING
200g/7oz/generous 1 cup cooked
stoned prunes
10ml/2 tsp grated lemon rind
5ml/1 tsp grated orange rind
1.5ml/¼ tsp grated nutmeg
40g/1½oz/3 tbsp butter, melted
50g/2oz/½ cup walnuts, very finely chopped
30ml/2 tbsp caster sugar

MAKES 1 LOAF

1 Melt the butter in the milk in a saucepan. Pour into a small jug and cool to hand-hot. Sift the flour into a large mixing bowl and stir in the salt, caster sugar and yeast.

2 Make a well in the centre of the dry ingredients and add the milk mixture, with the beaten egg. Mix in enough of the hand-hot water to make a soft dough. Knead on a lightly floured surface for about 10 minutes, until the dough is smooth and elastic. Return the dough to the clean bowl, cover with a dish cloth and leave in a warm place to rise for about 1½ hours or until doubled in bulk.

3 Lightly grease a large baking sheet. Make the filling by mixing all the ingredients in a bowl. When the dough is ready, punch it down, then roll it out on a lightly floured surface to a rectangle measuring 38 x 25cm/15 x 10in. Transfer to the baking sheet.

4 Spread the filling in the centre of the dough. Cut strips at an angle on either side of the filling, fold up one end neatly, then bring alternate strips up over the filling to make the plait. Tuck the excess dough underneath at the ends, to neaten.

5 Cover the plait loosely and leave in a warm place to rise again. Preheat the oven to 190°C/375°F/ Gas 5. Glaze the plait with the egg wash and bake for 30 minutes or until golden. Cool on a wire rack.

Swedish Sultana Bread

INGREDIENTS

175ml / 6fl oz / ¾ cup milk
150ml / ¼ pint / ⅔ cup water
15ml / 1 tbsp clear honey
225g / 8oz / 2 cups wholemeal flour
225g / 8oz / 2 cups strong white flour
5ml / 1 tsp salt
10ml / 2 tsp easy-blend dried yeast
115g / 4oz / ⅔ cup sultanas
50g / 2oz / ½ cup chopped walnuts
milk, for glazing

MAKES 1 LOAF

42

1 Bring the milk and water to simmering point in a small saucepan. Stir in the honey until dissolved, then pour the milk mixture into a jug and cool to hand-hot.

2 Sift both types of flour into a mixing bowl. Stir in the salt, yeast and sultanas. Set aside 15ml / 1 tbsp of the walnuts and add the rest to the bowl. Mix lightly. Make a well in the centre of the dry ingredients.

3 Add the hand-hot liquid to the well and mix to a soft dough. Add a little extra hand-hot water if necessary. Knead the dough on a lightly floured surface for 10 minutes, making sure that the dried fruit and nuts are well distributed.

4 Lightly grease a baking sheet. Pat the dough into a 28cm / 11in long sausage and place it on the baking sheet. Make about four diagonal cuts down the length.

5 Slide the baking sheet into a lightly oiled plastic bag. Leave the bread to rise in a warm place for about 1½ hours. Preheat the oven to 220°C / 425°F / Gas 7.

6 Brush the dough with milk, sprinkle it with the reserved walnuts and bake for 10 minutes. Lower the oven temperature to 200°C / 400°F / Gas 6 and bake for 20 minutes more. Cool on a wire rack.

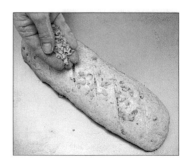

Lemon & Walnut Teabread

INGREDIENTS

*115g/4oz/½ cup butter or margarine, at
room temperature
115g/4oz/½ cup granulated sugar
2 eggs, separated
grated rind of 2 lemons
30ml/2 tbsp lemon juice
225g/8oz/2 cups plain flour
10ml/2 tsp baking powder
120–150ml/4–5fl oz/½–⅔ cup milk
50g/2oz/½ cup chopped walnuts
pinch of salt*

MAKES 1 LOAF

1 Preheat the oven to 180°C/350°F/Gas 4.
Grease a 450g/1lb loaf tin and base line it with
non-stick baking paper.

2 Cream the butter or margarine with the sugar
until light and fluffy. Beat in the egg yolks, then stir
in the lemon rind and juice.

3 In another bowl, sift the flour and baking powder together three times. Fold into the creamed
mixture in three batches, alternating with
120ml/4fl oz/½ cup of the milk. Fold in the
walnuts. The mixture should be quite stiff; add the
extra milk only if absolutely necessary.

4 Whisk the egg
whites with the
salt in a bowl until
stiff. Fold half the
egg white into the
walnut mixture to
lighten it, then
fold in the rest
until just mixed.

5 Spoon the mixture into the prepared tin. Bake
for 45 minutes or until a thin skewer inserted in
the teabread comes out clean. Cool on a wire rack.

Cranberry & Orange Bread

INGREDIENTS

225g/8oz/2 cups plain flour
10ml/2 tsp baking powder
115g/4oz/½ cup caster sugar
2.5ml/½ tsp salt
grated rind of 1 large orange
175ml/6fl oz/¾ cup orange juice
2 eggs, lightly beaten
75g/3oz/6 tbsp butter, melted
115g/4oz/1 cup fresh cranberries or bilberries
50g/2oz/½ cup chopped walnuts

MAKES 1 LOAF

1 Preheat the oven to 180°C/350°F/Gas 4. Grease a 450g/1lb loaf tin and base line it with non-stick baking paper.

2 Sift the flour and baking powder into a mixing bowl. Stir in the caster sugar, salt and orange rind. Make a well in the centre and add the orange juice, eggs and melted butter. Stir from the centre until the ingredients are just blended; do not overmix.

3 Add the berries and walnuts and stir gently until just mixed. Spread the mixture in the tin and bake for 45–50 minutes until the loaf is golden and the surface springs back when lightly touched with a finger.

4 Cool the bread in the tin for 10 minutes, then transfer to a wire rack to cool completely. Serve thinly sliced, with butter or cream cheese and jam.

Banana & Cardamom Bread

INGREDIENTS

350ml/12fl oz/1½ cups milk
good pinch of saffron strands
30ml/2 tbsp clear honey, plus extra
for glazing
2 ripe bananas
45ml/3 tbsp caster sugar
900g/2lb/8 cups strong white flour
5ml/1 tsp salt
25g/1oz/2 tbsp butter
2 x 10g/¼oz sachets easy-blend dried yeast
seeds from 6 cardamom pods
115g/4oz/⅔ cup raisins

MAKES 2 LOAVES

1 Heat the milk in a saucepan to simmering point. Pour a little into a cup and crumble in the saffron strands. Set aside to infuse for 5 minutes. Stir the

honey into the remaining milk, pour into a jug and cool to hand-hot. Using a fork, mash the bananas with the caster sugar.

2 Mix the flour and salt in a bowl. Rub in the butter until the mixture resembles breadcrumbs, then stir in the yeast and cardamom seeds.

3 Make a well in the centre and strain in the saffron milk. Add the honey-flavoured milk, mashed banana mixture and raisins. Mix to a soft dough. Add more hand-hot milk, if necessary.

4 Lightly grease two 450g/1lb loaf tins. Knead the dough on a lightly floured surface for 10 minutes. Divide the dough in half and fit each half into a loaf tin.

5 Slip the tins into a lightly oiled plastic bag and leave the loaves to rise for about 1½ hours until they have doubled in bulk. Preheat the oven to 200°C/400°F/Gas 6.

6 Bake the loaves for 20 minutes, then lower the oven temperature to 180°C/350°F/Gas 4 and bake for 20–25 minutes more, or until they sound hollow when rapped underneath. Place on wire racks and brush the tops with honey while the loaves are still warm.

46

Malt Loaf

INGREDIENTS

150ml/¼ pint/⅔ cup milk
45ml/3 tbsp malt extract
350g/12oz/3 cups plain flour
2.5ml/½ tsp salt
10g/¼oz sachet easy-blend dried yeast
30ml/2 tbsp light muscovado sugar
175g/6oz/1 cup sultanas
15ml/1 tbsp sunflower oil
GLAZE
30ml/2 tbsp caster sugar
30ml/2 tbsp water

MAKES 1 LOAF

1 Grease a 450g/1lb loaf tin. Heat the milk in a saucepan to simmering point. Stir in the malt extract until dissolved. Set aside to cool to hand-hot.

2 Mix the flour, salt, yeast and sugar in a bowl. Stir in the sultanas. Make a well in the centre and add the milk mixture and oil. Mix to a soft dough, adding more hand-hot milk if necessary.

3 Knead the dough on a lightly floured surface for 10 minutes, until smooth and elastic. Fit it in the loaf tin, cover and leave in a warm place to rise for about 1½ hours until it has doubled in bulk. Preheat the oven to 190°C/375°F/Gas 5.

4 Bake the loaf for 30 minutes, until it sounds hollow when rapped underneath. Meanwhile make the glaze. Dissolve the caster sugar in the water in a small pan. Bring to the boil, stirring, then lower the heat and simmer for 1 minute.

5 Put the loaf on a wire rack and brush it with the glaze while still hot. Leave the loaf to cool. Serve with butter and a fruit jam, if liked.

VARIATION

Make malt buns by dividing the loaf into 10 pieces, shaping them into rounds and leaving them to rise. Bake the buns for 15 minutes, then glaze.

Date & Pecan Loaf

INGREDIENTS

175g/6oz/1 cup stoned dates, chopped
175ml/6fl oz/³⁄4 cup boiling water
175g/6oz/1¹⁄2 cups plain flour
10ml/2 tsp baking powder
2.5ml/¹⁄2 tsp salt
1.5ml/¹⁄4 tsp grated nutmeg
50g/2oz/¹⁄4 cup butter, at room temperature
50g/2oz/¹⁄3 cup soft dark brown sugar
50g/2oz/¹⁄4 cup caster sugar
1 egg, lightly beaten
30ml/2 tbsp brandy
75g/3oz/³⁄4 cup chopped pecan nuts

MAKES 1 LOAF

1 Place the dates in a heatproof bowl and pour over the boiling water. Set aside to cool. Meanwhile preheat the oven to 180°C/350°F/Gas 4. Then grease a

450g/1lb loaf tin and base line with non-stick baking paper.

2 Sift the flour, baking powder and salt together. Add the nutmeg. Cream the butter with the sugars in a mixing bowl until light and fluffy. Beat in the egg and brandy.

3 Fold the dry ingredients into the creamed mixture in three batches, alternating with the dates (and soaking water).

4 Fold the chopped pecans into the mixture, scrape it into the tin and level the surface. Bake for 45–50 minutes or until a skewer inserted in the loaf comes out clean. Cool in the tin for 10 minutes before transferring to a wire rack to cool completely.

Spicy Apple Loaf

INGREDIENTS

1 egg
250ml / 8fl oz / 1 cup bottled or homemade
apple sauce
50g / 2oz / ¼ cup butter, melted
115g / 4oz / ⅔ cup soft dark brown sugar
50g / 2oz / ¼ cup caster sugar
275g / 10oz / 2½ cups plain flour
10ml / 2 tsp baking powder
2.5ml / ½ tsp bicarbonate of soda
2.5ml / ½ tsp salt
5ml / 1 tsp ground cinnamon
2.5ml / ½ tsp grated nutmeg
75g / 3oz / ½ cup currants or raisins
50g / 2oz / ½ cup chopped walnuts

MAKES 1 LOAF

2 Sift the flour, baking powder, bicarbonate of soda and salt into a separate bowl. Stir in the cinnamon and nutmeg. Add the dry ingredients to the apple sauce mixture in three batches, beating after each addition.

3 Stir in the dried fruit and nuts until evenly distributed. Scrape the mixture into the tin, level the surface and bake for about 1 hour or until a skewer inserted in the loaf comes out clean. Cool on a wire rack. Serve sliced, with butter.

1 Preheat the oven to 180°C/350°F/ Gas 4. Grease a 450g/1lb loaf tin and base line with non-stick baking paper. Beat the egg with the apple sauce, butter and both sugars in a mixing bowl. Set aside.

Flatbreads, Sticks & Rolls

Naan

INGREDIENTS

450g / 1lb / 4 cups plain flour
5ml / 1 tsp baking powder
2.5ml / ½ tsp salt
10ml / 2 tsp easy-blend dried yeast
175ml / 6fl oz / ¾ cup hand-hot milk
150ml / ¼ pint / ⅔ cup natural yogurt
1 egg, beaten
25g / 1oz / 2 tbsp ghee, melted, plus extra for greasing
chopped fresh coriander and onion seeds (kalonji) for the topping

MAKES 6–8

1 Mix the flour, baking powder, salt and yeast in a mixing bowl. Make a well in the centre and add the milk, yogurt, egg and ghee. Mix to a soft dough. Lightly grease 3–4 large baking sheets.

2 Knead the dough on a lightly floured surface for 10 minutes, until smooth and elastic. Divide into 6–8 balls and roll each one out to about 25cm/10in long and 15cm/6in wide, tapering to 5cm/2in.

3 Place the naan on the baking sheets, cover and leave to rise in a warm place for about 1 hour or until they have almost doubled in bulk. Preheat the oven to 200°C/400°F/Gas 6.

4 Sprinkle the naan with coriander and onion seeds (kalonji). Bake for 10 minutes until well risen and golden. Decorate with foil, if liked. Serve warm.

COOK'S TIP

Ghee is clarified butter. To make it at home, melt butter in a small pan, leave it to stand until the solids settle, then carefully pour off the clear yellow liquid ghee.

Focaccia

INGREDIENTS

400g/14oz/3½ cups strong white flour
5ml/1 tsp salt
10g/¼oz sachet easy-blend dried yeast
250ml/8fl oz/1 cup hand-hot water
75ml/5 tbsp olive oil
10ml/2 tsp coarse sea salt for the topping

MAKES 1 LOAF

1 Mix the flour, salt and yeast in a large bowl. Make a well in the centre and add the hand-hot water, with 30ml/2 tbsp of the oil. Mix to a soft dough, adding more hand-hot water if needed.

2 Transfer the dough to a lightly floured surface. Knead for 10 minutes, until smooth and elastic. Brush a 25cm/10in tart tin or pizza pan lightly with oil.

3 Press the dough into the tin, cover and leave in a warm place for about 1 hour or until doubled in bulk. Preheat the oven to 200°C/400°F/Gas 6.

4 Using your fingers, dimple the dough all over. Pour the remaining oil over the dough and brush it to the edges. Sprinkle with the coarse sea salt.

5 Bake in the preheated oven for 20–25 minutes until the bread is pale gold. Allow to cool slightly on a wire rack before serving.

COOK'S TIP
Focaccia is best eaten on the day it is made but it also freezes very well and can be prepared in advance for entertaining.

Cheese & Onion Herb Sticks

INGREDIENTS

15ml/1 tbsp sunflower oil
1 red onion, finely chopped
450g/1lb/4 cups strong white flour
5ml/1 tsp salt
7.5ml/1½ tsp easy-blend dried yeast
5ml/1 tsp mustard powder
45ml/3 tbsp chopped fresh herbs, such as
thyme, parsley, marjoram or sage
75g/3oz/¾ cup grated mature Cheddar cheese
300ml/½ pint/1¼ cups hand-hot water

MAKES 2 STICKS

1 Heat the oil in a frying pan and fry the onion until golden brown. Mix the flour, salt, yeast, mustard powder and chopped herbs in a bowl. Set 30ml/2 tbsp of the cheese aside; add the rest to the bowl.

2 Make a well in the centre of the flour mixture and add the onion (with the oil) and the water. Mix to a soft dough. Grease two baking sheets.

3 Knead the dough on a lightly floured surface for 10 minutes, or until smooth and elastic. Divide it in half. Roll each piece to a 30cm/12in stick. Place each stick on a baking sheet, cover and leave to rise in a warm place for 1 hour, or until well risen.

4 Preheat the oven to 220°C/425°F/Gas 7. Place each stick on a baking sheet and make diagonal cuts along the top. Sprinkle with the reserved cheese. Bake for 25 minutes or until the sticks sound hollow when rapped underneath. Cool on a wire rack.

VARIATION

To make Onion and Coriander Sticks, omit the cheese, herbs and mustard. Add 15ml/1 tbsp ground coriander and 45ml/3 tbsp chopped fresh coriander instead.

Italian Breadsticks

INGREDIENTS

120ml/4fl oz/½ cup water
10ml/2 tsp malt extract
225g/8oz/2 cups strong white flour
5ml/1 tsp salt
5ml/1 tsp easy-blend dried yeast
poppy seeds, see method

MAKES ABOUT 30

1 Heat the water in a small pan. Stir in the malt extract until dissolved. Pour into a jug and cool to hand-hot.

2 Mix the flour, salt and yeast in a bowl. Make a well in the centre and add the hand-hot liquid. Mix to a firm dough, then knead on a lightly floured surface for 10 minutes, until smooth and elastic. Shape the dough into a ball.

3 Tear off a walnut-sized lump of dough and roll it into a small sausage shape. Repeat with the remaining dough to make about 30 pieces in all. Lightly grease four baking sheets.

4 On an unfloured surface, roll a piece of dough with your fingers to make a stick about 9mm/¾in thick. Repeat with the rest of the dough. Roll some of the sticks in  poppy seeds, then place them on the baking sheets. Cover and leave to rise in a warm place for about 15 minutes. Preheat the oven to 200°C/400°F/Gas 6.

5 Bake the bread sticks for 8–10 minutes, then turn them over and bake for 6–7 minutes more. Do not let them brown. Cool on wire racks.

Granary Baps

INGREDIENTS

300ml / ½ pint / 1¼ cups water
15ml / 1 tbsp malt extract
450g / 1lb / 4 cups malted brown flour
5ml / 1 tsp salt
5ml / 1 tsp easy-blend dried yeast
15ml / 1 tbsp rolled oats

MAKES 8

58

1 Heat the water in a saucepan to simmering point. Dissolve the malt extract, then cool to hand-hot.

2 Mix the flour, salt and yeast in a bowl. Make a well in the centre and add the hand-hot liquid. Mix to a soft dough, then knead on a lightly floured surface for 10 minutes, until smooth and elastic.

3 Divide the dough into eight pieces and shape each to a ball. Flatten the balls with the palm of your hand to make neat 10cm/4in rounds. Lightly grease a large baking sheet.

4 Place the rounds on the baking sheet, cover loosely with a large, lightly oiled plastic bag (ballooning it to trap the air inside) and leave in a warm place for about 1 hour or until the baps have almost doubled in size. Preheat the oven to 220°C/425°F/Gas 7.

5 Brush the baps with water, sprinkle with the oats and bake for 20–25 minutes or until they sound hollow when rapped underneath. Cool on a wire rack, then serve with your favourite filling.

COOK'S TIP
The same amount of mixture can be used to make about a dozen smaller rolls, if prefered.

Dinner Milk Rolls

INGREDIENTS

675g / 1½lb / 6 cups strong plain flour
10ml / 2 tsp salt
25g / 1oz / 2 tbsp butter
10g / ¼oz sachet easy-blend dried yeast
about 450ml / ¾ pint / 1¾ cups hand-hot milk
cold milk, for glazing
poppy, sesame and sunflower seeds or sea salt flakes, for the topping

MAKES 12–16

1 Sift the flour and salt into a large bowl. Rub in the butter, then stir in the yeast. Make a well in the centre and add enough of the hand-hot milk to make a soft dough.

2 Knead the dough on a lightly floured surface for 10 minutes, or until smooth and elastic. Shape into 12–16 rounds or fun shapes, such as knots or mini cottage loaves. Lightly grease two baking sheets.

3 Place the shapes on the baking sheet, cover and leave in a warm place for about 1 hour or until they have doubled in size. Preheat the oven to 230°C/450°F/Gas 8.

4 Glaze the rolls with milk and sprinkle over your chosen topping. Bake for 12 minutes, until the rolls are golden brown and cooked. Cool on a wire rack.

COOK'S TIP

These rolls are best eaten on the day they are made. Serve them just warm, if possible.

Individual Brioches

INGREDIENTS

200g/7oz/1¾ cups plain flour
2.5ml/½ tsp salt
15ml/1 tbsp caster sugar
10g/¼oz sachet easy-blend dried yeast
30ml/2 tbsp hand-hot milk
2 eggs, lightly beaten
*75g/3oz/6 tbsp butter, diced, at room
temperature*
*1 egg yolk, beaten with 10ml/2 tsp water,
for glazing*

MAKES 8

1 Lightly butter eight individual brioche tins or muffin tins. Put the flour, salt, sugar and yeast in a food processor.

2 With the machine running, add the hand-hot milk and eggs through the feeder tube, until combined. Scrape down the sides and process for 2–3 minutes more, or

until the dough forms a ball. Add the butter and pulse about 10 times until it is fully incorporated.

3 Shape three quarters of the dough into eight balls and put in the prepared tins. Shape the remaining dough into smaller balls. Make a dent in each large ball and centre a small ball on top. Cover and leave the brioches to rise in a warm place for about 1 hour, until doubled in size. Preheat the oven to 200°C/400°F/Gas 6.

4 Brush the brioches lightly with the egg wash and bake for 15–18 minutes until golden brown. Cool on a wire rack.

61

Croissants

INGREDIENTS

500g / 1¼lb / 5 cups plain flour
7.5ml / 1½ tsp salt
10ml / 2 tsp caster sugar
15ml / 1 tbsp easy-blend dried yeast
325ml / 11fl oz / 1⅓ cups hand-hot milk
225g / 8oz / 1 cup cold butter
1 egg, beaten with 10ml / 2 tsp water, for glazing

MAKES 18

1 Mix the flour, salt, sugar and yeast in a large bowl. Make a well in the centre and add enough of the hand-hot milk to make a soft dough. Return to a clean bowl, cover and leave in a warm place for about 1½ hours, until doubled in bulk.

2 Knead the dough until smooth. Wrap in grease-proof paper and chill for 15 minutes. Meanwhile, divide the butter in half and roll each half between two sheets of greaseproof paper to form a 15 x 10cm/6 x 4in rectangle.

3 On a floured surface, roll out the dough to a 30 x 20cm/12 x 8in rectangle. Place a sheet of butter in the centre. Fold the bottom third of dough over the butter, press to seal, then place the remaining butter sheet on top. Fold over the top third.

4 Turn the dough so the short side faces you. Roll it gently to a 30 x 20cm/12 x 8in rectangle. Fold in thirds as before, then wrap and chill for 30 min-

utes. Repeat this process twice more, then wrap and chill for at least 2 hours, or overnight.

5 Roll out the dough to a thin rectangle, about 33cm/13in wide. Cut in half, then into triangles, 15cm/6in high, with a 10cm/4in base. Roll the tri-

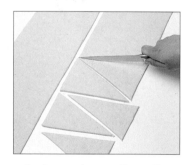

angles slightly to stretch them, then roll up from base to point. Place on baking sheets, curving to make crescents. Cover and leave in a warm place for 1–1½ hours or until more than doubled in size. Preheat the oven to 240°C/475°F/Gas 9.

6 Brush the croissants with the egg wash and bake for 2 minutes. Lower the oven temperature to 190°C/375°F/Gas 5 and bake for 10–12 minutes more, until golden. Serve warm.

Index